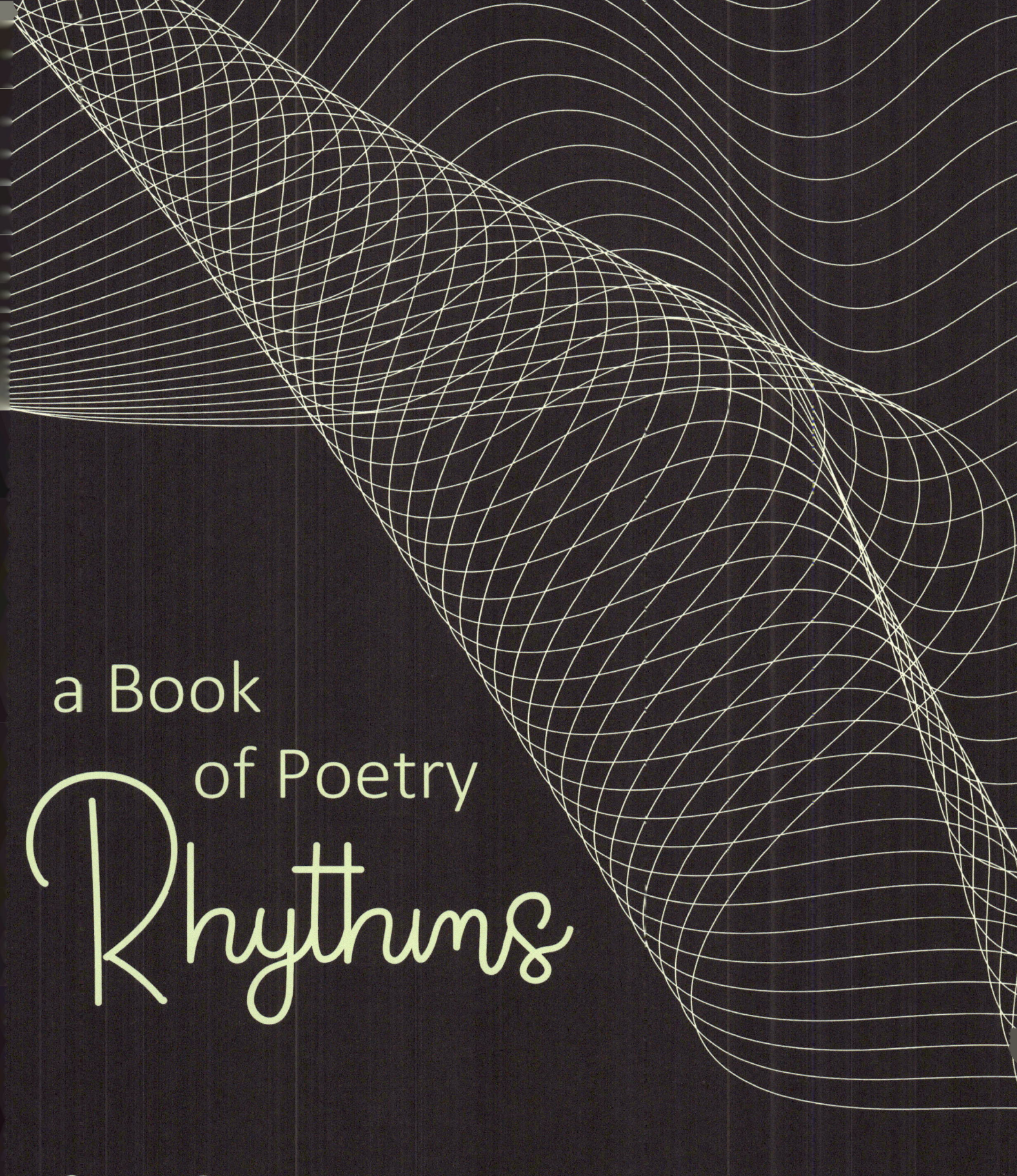

a Book
of Poetry
Rhythms

Queen Roshaunda

WORKBOOK PRESS LLC
187 E Warm Springs Rd,
Suite B285, Las Vegas, NV 89119, USA

Website: https://workbookpress.com/
Hotline: 1-888-818-4856
Email: admin@workbookpress.com

Ordering Information:
Quantity sales. Special discounts are available on quantity purchases by corporations, associations, and others.
For details, contact the publisher at the address above.

Library of Congress Control Number:
ISBN-13: 978-1-953839-20-6 (Paperback Version)
          978-1-953839-22-0 (Digital Version)

REV. DATE: 09/26/2022

A Book of Poetry Rhythms

Written by:

Queen Roshaunda

Introduction

A Book Of Poetry Rhythms

Peace and blessings for god beautiful creation, and for all those who have been blessed with their hands by touching this book of poetry. Poetry has a profound way of reaching our hearts, minds, and souls. The creator inspired my words of wisdom as well as to understand why I choose to write on these different to-pics of rhythms. It is very important for all humans to understand why we move around the way we do, and why it is important to know how to move around as who you represent yourself to be. Your energy represents a statement of truth, however the way you move around is a linked energy connected to your statements made by your rhythm.

Ten years of research, and of now being blessed with understanding pertaining to what rhythm is all about. I have found out that rhythm is more important than most of us would imagine it to be. I have interviewed daughters of mothers who always complained about how their mothers don't understand them. On the other hand, mothers were complaining about how their mothers don't understand them. As well as their daughters never listening to them and of why their daughters won't clean up their rooms, not doing what is expected of them which links mothers and daughters to know clear understanding of their own personal connection with their rhythms, then I interviewed fathers complaining about their son's sons complaining about their father's, husbands complaining about their wife, or wives. Sister's having dissatisfaction about their communication with their sister.

Cousins unpleased about their connection with other cousins not demonstrating the ships of cousin bonding. The list goes on and on. Uncles displeased sending negative energy out about nieces and nephews, brothers complaining brothers. There's even more dissatisfaction in are royal families, the prince upset about how the princess is caring out her everyday acts. Rings are always complaining about queens not listening and following instructions, queens upset with the king's for lieing so much not arriving on time for important functions. So, I, queen Roshaunda have been inspired to write this book of pods to bring clarity and strong understanding pertaining to this topic "RHYTHMS" of what it's all about.

Peace To All

Queen Roshaunda

Butterfly Love

Never Give Up!

"A Book of Poetry Rhythms"

It's time to sit down and think for a moment about these titles of anointments that are pass

down the family trees of precious life.

Rhythm is I, rhythm is in you

Rhythm is in the universe,

rhythm is in motion, without

movement how would the world keep moving, keep evolving.

Guess what! Without rhythm we

would be motionless

"CONTENTS"

The Rhythm Of A Cousin   10

The Rhythm Of A Strong Prince   11

The Rhythm Of A Woman   12

The Rhythm Of A Man   13

The Rhythm Of A Beautiful Princess   14

The Rhythm Of A Nurturing Mother   15

The Rhythm Of A Strong And Protective Father   16

The Rhythm Of A Grandmother   17

The Rhythm Of A Grandfather   18

The Rhythm Of An Uncle   19

The Rhythm Of An Aunt   20

The Rhythm Of A Real Sister   21

The Rhythm Of A Real Brother   22

The Rhythm Of A Nephew   23

The Rhythm Of A King   24

The Rhythm Of A Queen   25

The Rhythm Of A Niece   26

The Rhythm Of A Wife   27

The Rhythm Of A Husband   28

The Rhythm Of A Friend   29

"The Rhythm Of A Cousin"

I welcome you with joy when you visit, I am happy to see you. You look beautiful, how do you feel? Would you like a cup of tea, or a glass of wine! What's been going on these days? Have you been out wining and dining, because you sure are shinning. I always knew that you were a star always bright as the sun full of light and laughter. No matter what was said about you. I remained to know that I should always respect you just because you are alive ready at all times to dive into I, something about you cousin just being around you makes the time pass by so quick. We don't talk about one another, we are real with one another, we can talk about each other face to face, and then laugh and go on are marry way and quote peace! Are bond for real? We don't communicate in a back stabbing drama way, that energy is out in the ruff and tuff dirty streets. we keep it straight up with one another, you no real! face to face, one on one, close up, eye to eye, because whatever we bring to the table that need to be discussed is all about truth rather it hurt, or feel as pain we choke it up and move on next. You are always down with I we have each other's back if we need to scream at each other to get a statement across will do just that. We understand that real love is always going to be put to test. However, from both of us having real understanding about what being a real cousin is. We know we will always be strong for each other just because we are cousins. "The Rhythm Of A Cousin".

Written By Queen Roshaunda
Real Cousins Respect One Another Always

"The Rhythm Of A Strong Prince"

I am bold. I am here. I run wild sometime; God made I this way. lam the prince. You know sometime I just have to watch out for that tree! Remember I am the prince fast, quick, swift, and I can move in all directions just because I am the prince God made I to be this way. I am not bad Ian just brave with no fear, I am the prince. I run let I play its okay Tam just being that ruler that enjoys moving in the rhythm and fashion as the prince. Take it slow think it, think it slow and understand who I am the prince. Learn to observe watch a little closer, focus more into my eyes my soul and maybe you might see that this is my rhythm. "The Rhythm Of A Strong Prince".

Written By Queen Roshaunda
Dedicated to Little Prince Nigel

"The Rhythm Of A Woman"

The rhythm of a woman is like keeping up with a train in motion called action in thought. If you can run you can relate, or you will get left behind. She stays tuned with her rhythm bringing all her desires into her dynamic driving force of power which equal into her reality. When she dances in your life you will feel the vibration of soul. When you look in her eyes you will see the symbols of music flash through your eyes. The movement in her walk is like the sound of thunder which connects her to the sound of funk. Her rhythm is so strong she even dances to her own soul feeling her rhythm in motion. Her rhythm will question you how long can you dance, can you keep up with my beat, or will I have to slow down, I don't think so. Can you move to my beat, or will I have to drag you along to my beat? If you have understanding of who tam, you will know Tam your rhythm. The mother of civilization.

Written By Queen Roshaunda

"The Rhythm Of A Man"

We can go this way, or that way. It depends on you to let me know if you can flow, because as of right now I am going this way, the straight path of clearness, I need to see clear at all times, not just for right now, but forever a lasting light. Make a way for me I don't need nothing behind just on the side. I am asking for balance, that's not asking for too much. Just don't rush I, because I am smooth, I can handle this just deal with me don't fight it, try to understand this rhythm it's no joke it's for real, so you better be able to understand and deal with where I am coming from. My rhythm is law competent; you know strong so you see, you can't play with this rhythm because if so, you will feel the strike, you will know I was there, and wake up and say dame where did that rhythm go?

Written By Queen Roshaunda

"The Rhythm Of A Beautiful Princess"

The rhythm of a princess. I want this now I give it now. I don't want to wait; don't you understand god wants I to live in the now the present moment always. Mommy and daddy don't get upset with me, because I live in the present moment it's all because I am small and ram only going to be a princess now, if you just let, I live in the now maybe I will show you how to live in the now.

Written By Queen Roshaunda
Dedicated To My beautiful daughter Ameerah Naajidah Bilal
Who Love Being Who She Is A PRINCESS

"The Rhythm Of A Nurturing Mother"

The rhythm of a nurturing mom is soft spoken and kind, but also wise she does not mind doing for her family and helping her love ones become the best that they can be in life. The nurturing mother has concern for all those who are around her, as well as concern for her environment. The rhythm of a nurturing mother is always aware she knows and understands why she must watch and view close range at all situations. She enjoys helping others and making sure that others understand why they should and suppose to help others. Her rhythm is together accurate, correct, at all times. Her motion is in connection a oneness with god her higher power. The nurturing mother loves to please her love ones at all times she knows it will return to her more in many ways. The nurturing mother has no time to play foolish games with others. Her rhythm comes and moves in a correct proper fashion knowing she is a motion connected to truth and honesty. Her rhythm is of thoughtfulness sweetness, but most of all the rhythm of a nurturing mother, most important task is for her to find, and keep god in the center of her life always.

Written By Queen Roshaunda

Dedicated to My Beautiful and Kind Mother,
Mrs. Shirley Alexander

"The Rhythm Of A Strong Protective Father"

My rhythm is strong, hard for real. You know I am a provider, so you see I have no choice, I have to be serious and conduct myself in a serious stern way. My rhythm is law it's in connection with the ten commandments. I must obey god's rhythm which only strengthens my rhythm into firmness Iam on the move in motion going out everyday as a hunter returning home in a relax manner waiting and ready to be served as a provider, then who takes his rhythm home because you see my rhythm don't have time to play games either you understand Iam for real, or you get ran over by my strength. My rhythm is bold, it doesn't unfold unless the power of God releases it to do so, otherwise I just rool as if I was bowling in a control smooth way. I am made to protect and serve those who are connected to I in the spiritual realm of truth righteousness, that's right understand what Iam saying only those who search and yearns to keep a connection with truth honesty and strive every-day to live in the world of truth. all Iam saying out loud is when you step to this strength you better come clean correct and quick, but last most important is you have no choice but to come real if not you just won't get in.

Written By Queen Roshaunda
Dedicated to my Dad, Thaddis Alexander
And to All Strong and Protective
Dads Around the World

"The Rhythm Of A Grandmother"

Come on in, Sam happy to see you. Don't stay away so long grandma misses you, I baked your favorite apple pie just because I knew you were coming over. Look at you looking so good! Keep taking care of yourself! Always save some money, and remember you deserve the best I prepared some dinner for you, you are always welcomed to visit are house, if you ever need a place to stay to help yourself get up to go back out in the world to do battle you can always return to grandma rhythm remember I am made to stand by your side. Just remember there are wolves out there, but they can't bite you if you are always doing the right thing in your life. Stay connected to god everything else will work its way out the way it's supposed to be done. Be brave have courage you can do whatever you set your mind to accomplish don't take too much, balance your thinking so you can achieve what you need to achieve. Bring all your dreams into your reality. Stay focus and remember it's better that you do what's right in life, I know I talk a lot, however remember that this is just, "The Rhythm Of A Grandma".

Written By Queen Roshaunda
Dedicated to both of my Grandmothers from mother and father's sides
Josephine Lundie

"The Rhythm Of A Grandfather"

Come on in here! I am happy to see you, are you making any money? How much you have in those pockets, give me five-dollars, I changed my mind give me a hundred dollars! How much you spending on that bottle of wine come on in. Give me half, take your hat off when you come in this house that's what the hat racks are for. Take your coat off hang it up. Set down for a moment know need to rush be happy that your here. come again see you next time. The Rhythm of A Grandfather straight, direct, you know strictly business!

Written By Queen Roshaunda
Dedicated to Grandpa
Will Always be Remembered

"The Rhythm Of An Uncle"

You know I Respect you, because of who you are. I tell you sometime be quiet don't talk too much; listen to this wisdom I have to give you. My rhythm as an uncle informs I to let you know how serious it is for you to listen close and understand what I am speaking to you. This is my responsibility. I am your uncle. Play your cards right in life, always strive to win. Today is your birthday here's a hundred-dollars by yourself something special. Remember to take care of yourself don't behave, or act stupid in the madness out in the world, hold your head up high think about what you are doing at all times. I am your uncle I wouldn't tell you nothing wrong just learn to listen more have a seat at the dinner table have dinner with I more often. What are your plans in life, behave in the right manner at all times. If you need to stay with your uncle to get your goals straight, I welcome you, you can stay as long as you keep working toward what you are doing, I will never kick you out in the streets, or say you have to move before you are ready to move just take your time save yourself some money. Don't worry I will not talk down on you because you're staying in my house. I am not connected to this house I am only connected to god which gives I strength to remain to always know what my role is to you. My rhythm is the rhythm of an uncle.

Written By Queen Roshaunda
Dedicated to my real true uncle who never crossed me
wrong in any way accept but in God's Way, "Uncle James"
He is known in the city of Phoenix, Arizona as one of the best football
players who has a plate of gold and an award for his good work.
Dedicated to my favorite Positive Uncle,
Aka Uncle Bobby Thomas/ Apostle

"The Rhythm Of An Aunt"

Come on in its such a pleasure seeing you, you look so well, how are you feeling you need some of these healthy vegetables and salad I am preparing. Sit down let I fix your plate. Your skin looks so healthy. I really do miss you don't stay away so long, I purchased you a gold necklace, and a diamond bracelet you deserve it. Iam your aunt I have something to be proud of because I understand who I am, I am connected to your rhythm the connection of what an aunt is, you mean more to me then this diamond bracelet, or necklace. I am just demonstrating who I am. I am your aunt; just never forget it this is my rhythm.

Written By Queen Roshaunda

Dedicated to Aunt Joy
And All other
Beautiful Aunts in the World

"The Rhythm Of A Sister"

The rhythm of a sister respects her sister she understands the bond they share is from god she enjoys helping it's a pleasure for her to be able to help when she needs the support. A sister loves her sister just because she's special! "The Rhythm Of A Sister" is always there for you, if you need a favorite, you can always depend on the rhythm of a sister, she does for another with pleasure no matter how difficult the task may be just because she is able to be around her sister. The rhythm of a sister is straight and direct with you, she doesn't run out in the world and spread gossip she knows that she does not have to talk about you behind your back. A sister communicate face to face with you. A sister doesn't question why you need a ride she just drives you there if you need her help. A sister rhythm is of help at all times because she knows what's important, she does not want to ever lose the sister connection because there's just something special about sisters no matter what happens a sister is always there for you.

Written By Queen Roshaunda
Dedicated to
All Sisters in the World

"The Rhythm Of A Brother"

Come here now, because I told you so, slow down take your time why are you trying to rush me. hand me my brush that's my pie in the refrigerator don't eat it all, you can have a slice. Where leaving right now, not when you want to when I say where going to leave, we leave at my command. "The Rhythm Of A Brother" always demanding always bossing you around. A brother will protect you he's always by your side no matter what he questions who's at the door what do they want he may let you in, or may not it just depend if he thinks your cool if your cool it's okay, but if you are a fool the rhythm of a brother just don't have time to be fade it by the bull.

Written By Queen Roshaunda

Dedicated to all brothers in the world
Protect your seat and life
You are the best brother!

22

"The Rhythm Of A Nephew"

I know who you are I respect you your smart you stand for something move out my way let I learn so I can go out and earn. I am here now; what you think about me now can you understand what I am doing? Do you know where I am going in life, or are you just trying to get in and control my life like everybody else you have to explain yourself otherwise you stay out, or you might just end up chasing this rhythm like everybody else and end up just another being who ends up getting nothing from "The Rhythm Of A Nephew" You have to explain yourself otherwise you stay out, all I can say is just keep watching all eyes on my soul! Remember I told you I am somebody special just because tam who I am "The Rhythm Of A Nephew".

Written By Queen Roshaunda
Dedicated to Nephew Julies James Jefferson

"The Rhythm Of A King"

Here I come I am on my way bold and strong ready at all times to conquer, just because I can, my rhythm is king direct to the point. I arrive on time I have known time to waste I don't mess around in the world of foolishness. I show up when I say I am. I leave when it's time to leave. My rhythm is serious quick and most certainly alert at all times. I have to see and know what's going on around myself always. My rhythm is sharp flexible accurate right on time, either you can roll with this, or you get on. I am not trying to sound mean but you know this is just "The Rhythm Of A King" If I spoke in any other fashion or sound. I would not be behaving in this king manner. I know I walk with strength arriving in a just way of disposition of power one with discipline ready to give order my rhythm is always ready to instruct enforce show others into the light because this is what the true real bold king rhythm is all about. So now you know I said it this is what my rhythm is all about. "The Rhythm Of A King".

Written By Queen Roshaunda

Dedicated to All Powerful Kings on the Planet Earth!

"The Rhythm Of A Queen"

How do you do? Hello everyone! I have arrived. I move with grace poise and in a serene secure manner. My rhythm is queen you know sharp. I move in on you in style I move with grace although I glide away in a way of you not even recognizing I was there. That's just the way I am don't take it personal I am just who I am the queen the rhythm of balance of the entire universe. My rhythm is complete I am hold because god the creator glide through I making the queen walk in a harmony way gentle, smooth, very stealthily, gradually in motion as if her feet are walking through the clouds. That's right! This is that real rhythm of a queen. My rhythm is quick ready at all times to make righteous moves at all times on all high dimensions of life. The queen rhythm is serious carrying a disposition of earnest importance. Demonstrating harmonic poise from all different degrees of angles in just the way I move and c carry myself. That's why it's just know other who could ever den-ounce, or perpetrate this real rhythm of the queen who walks the earth.

Written By Queen Roshaunda
Dedicated to All Queen
Who refused and never give up

"The Rhythm Of A Niece"

Can I go with you? will you by me this, can I have some? You like my knew shoes? You look so pretty I want to be just like you when I grow up. I can dance so good can you do this knew dance, I can show you, I can teach you if you take the time and stop for a moment. I am your niece I am always excited to see you, you bring joy to my soul I look up to you I look forward to seeing you but please never forget I am your niece always. "The Rhythm Of A Niece ".

Written By Queen Roshaunda
Dedicated to All Rider Nieces!

"The Rhythm Of A Wife"

I am pleasant. I am loveably. I welcome you with joy. I walk in a graceful manner I move accordingly to the way god wants I to move my rhythm is clean neat my rhythm knows its importance, my rhythm makes moves in a just way doing what should be accomplished in a decent manner knowing this is, and the only way your rhythm should move. The rhythm of a wife is very cunning and wise what makes her rhythm of wisdom is because she knows that she must obey her creator which gives her wisdom to know how tasks are to be performed from her soul. A wife rhythm represents beauty she knows that its best to practice the art of honesty. Her rhythm is quiet at times she knows that most of the time it's better for her to listen to see and understand what is really trying to unravel its self into. which explains why a rhythm of a wife is truly earned to know and must always be respected and honored.

Written By Queen Roshaunda

"The Rhythm Of A Husband"

You recognize my rhythm you can here and feel this presence of a strong vibration who is secure from within shinning on to the outside of myself this rhythm is sharp quick it has no time to play games ready to make moves at all times, and always ready to bring order into all situations. This rhythm is powerful ready at times to provide assist, to help, to give, lead most of the time. I am called to take charge, because this is the rhythm of a husband being bold most of the time, this is just the way I am, this rhythm is of soundness ready on command to give orders to instruct and guide all into right conduct making moves always in a right conduct of fashion. This rhythm is cool at times calm collect as well, but powerful carrying know energy of fear just because god has given I this energy this rhythm I pronounce is the rhythm of a husband.

Written By Queen Roshaunda

"The Rhythm Of A Friend"

I need someone to listen to what I have to say right now! Of course, I can listen my rhythm is friendship when it's time for you to talk I listen. When it's time to make moves in the outside world we move in oneness because our rhythm of friendship is of connection based on honesty knowing that friendship can only stand and roll in a movement based upon truth. The rhythm of a friend is dependable moving quick doing what it has committed to do having strong concern of caring that this ship of friendship must be taking serious if it demonstrated, so just always remember "The Rhythm Of A Friend" is always, and always will be priceless. There's just know amount of money worth the life connection of real, pure, friendship.

Written By Queen Roshaunda

...THE END...

www.ingramcontent.com/pod-product-compliance
Lightning Source LLC
Chambersburg PA
CBHW041609120626
46551CB00002B/368